MW00874439

SAYING, "NO" TO THE INVITATION

Annaliza Moo Yin-McDaniels

Saying "No" to the Invitation

Copyright © 2019 by Annaliza Moo Yin-McDaniels

Unless otherwise indicated, all scriptural quotations are from the King James Version (KJV) of the Bible. All rights reserved.

According to the 1976 United States Copyright Act, no part of this book in whole or in part may be reproduced or transmitted in any form or by any means, electronic or mechanical, including photocopying, recording, or by any information storage and retrieval system, is permitted and is unlawful without the express written consent granted from the author.

All intellectual theft, phrases and ideas, are fully subject to the full prosecution of the law. For permissions, contact Mrs. Annaliza Moo Yin-McDaniels.

Name: Mrs. Annaliza Moo Yin-McDaniels

Email: SayingNoToTheInvitation@gmail.com

DEDICATION PAGE

I dedicate this book to my mother, Carol Moo Yin-Wood.

My mother influenced the writing of this book because she was a woman of faith and strength. My mother went through a lot of trials and testing and she walked away victorious every time. She was peace, she was love! If you were ever graced to be in her presence, her embrace alone was so calming and soothing; it always reassured me that everything was going to be alright. It would break so much off your life; it was as if you were going through deliverance when she wrapped her loving arms around you. She was the representation of the love that Jesus spoke about, the love that covers a multitude of sin, that love that covers all. I thank God he brought me back from Arizona so I was able to have that one on one mother daughter moments every day for 6 months while on our way to dropping her off and picking her up from work. It was as if God knew I needed to build that bond knowing she would soon be gone out of my life forever. I treasure every moment spent shopping and doing what she loved. I recall having various deep conversations, with my mom on my road to healing and freedom where I asked her numerous questions about our history: (1) Why she was the way she was and (2) I also inquired about possible generational/bloodline curses that seemed to plague our family.

My mom, Mrs. Carol Moo Yin-Wood, was very transparent about incest patterns on her father's bloodline, and she included other things on her mother's side too. My mom shared things she endured growing up in Jamaica, where she was molested repeatedly by a family member. It was then that I understood why my mother was extremely passive about certain issues.

When your voice is taken, it leaves many empty spaces in your life; certain behaviors will stem from that trauma. Until you are completely healed, you cannot have a voice for no one else, if you are still battling to speak for yourself. I gave her a hard time when I didn't understand why she was so passive and forgiving; I would constantly fight and defend her at all cost. I didn't care, even to the point of people disliking me for getting involved. I always felt I had to step in to defend her because she didn't know how to stand up for herself. (I am always trying to defend others, but couldn't stand up for self) After a long conversation one day my mother divulged all the abuse/pain and suffering she endured. (I experienced and watched a lot of the trauma and abuse first hand). I had to repent to her for not understanding her struggle, for not being sensitive to her pain. At that moment I finally understood her!

My mother endured physical and mental abuse, yet this woman remained strong! My mother was very forgiving, and her famous saying has always been, "God can take care of people better than you can!" And, she truly lived by that principle.

She allowed God to fight for her! I watched this beautiful loving woman walk out God's love towards everyone, even to the people that mistreated her.

My mother was taught to remain silent to keep peace no matter what she faced. She was strong and loving until the end, and I will stand strong and help others to walk in total healing like my mother did until I take that last breath.

My mom told me before she left this earth that she loved my strength and how I always fought for myself and others. Mom said she was so proud of the woman I became, and she wished she could have been as bold as I was. God is faithful to her prayers for her children. Remember God will always vindicate His children.

Rest in peace, to the beautiful woman I called mama, Mrs. Carol Moo Yin-Wood.

Know this, No matter what you face in life; God can heal your pain, seeking professional help and having a relationship with God are things which can be done to assist and accelerate the healing process...

He was wounded for our transgressions; he was bruised for our iniquities: the chastisement of our peace was upon him; and with his stripes we are healed. **Isaiah 53:5 (KJV)**

ACKNOWLEDGEMENT

I would like to acknowledge my husband, Sean McDaniels, for his love and support on my journey to complete my purpose in life. You keep me balanced and you complete me in so many ways. You came in my life to help me walk out my process to destiny. I love you baby!

My grandmother Cynthia Jackson, who worked hard to send us all to private school, while providing us with a better life. "Thank you for your sacrifice."

To my father, Henry Moo Yin. You have always been there for me whenever I needed you. You have always been a protector and a provider. You are my world greatest father and I couldn't imagine life without you in it.

To my other dad, David Wood, you too have been there, and your love language has always been your food. I love you for all you brought to my life.

I also acknowledge my siblings, Michael, Sheryl, Dave, Fianna, Christopher, and Brianna who walked with me through the road of trials and testing. You all loved me, even when I was not lovable; I love and appreciate you for keeping me on my toes.

To my children Zachaeus & Shiyane Phillips, you had to deal with a mother that had wounds from past hurts. As parents, we don't always have a blueprint, yet you loved me. You both will forever be my heartbeat. My challenge to you is to be greater than me. I attempted to pour plenty into you, so you will have fruit that will remain. I cannot wait to see Gods purpose for your life unfold, I expect nothing less than your absolute best!

To my other children, Lauren, Nia, Immanuel, and Imani, please remember that you have a voice and you should use it to speak up against any injustice or any unpleasant thing that comes your way.

To the amazing Caleb's, God has placed in my life, that helped me through some hard times on my road to healing, during their season or lifetime position in my life.

Jamila B, Michelle, Katina, Latoya, Jamila P, Faith, Antionette, and Demetra, you pushed me to never quit and to keep pressing toward the mark of the higher calling. You all sowed so much in my life at different season.

"Thank-You," to my cousin Candice and Dalmarie for always pushing me to be greater.

To Apostle Carlos & Pam Malone, thank-you for always encouraging and being there for me when I needed spiritual guidance.

To the grandbabies that I am working so hard to leave a legacy for, Aubrey, Amiya, Sumanie, and Shinyere, Grammy loves you!

Aunty Judy, "Thank-You" for your pour in my life.

To my Family...I love you guys! To everyone else that helped me in any way on my journey, I say a heartfelt, "Thank-You!"

To Kairos and Linda Jernigan, "Thank-You" for tapping into my vision for this amazing book cover.

FOREWORD

There are risks involved in mostly anything we do; but speaking out regarding personal molestation is a risk worth taking, and it takes *courage!*

It is amazing that it takes being a coward to rape someone but courage for a victim to report it. In this personal literary dossier, *Saying No to the Invitation*, my spiritual daughter, Annaliza Moo Yin-McDaniels shows courage, confidence and compassion as she tells her story and shares the story of other individuals whose lives were interrupted by the act of intrusion.

This book not only tells the stories of others, but it imparts methods of healings that can compel a person into the victory of overcoming the violation that interrupted their lives.

I encourage everyone to read this book and draw from the well of hope and encouragement, a refreshing new course towards peace beyond your pain. No longer should you mask your misery, but rather reach deep inside and discover the power that you possess to make the bold step that says, "I didn't ask for this, and I won't settle in it any longer!"

Apostle, Carlos L. Malone, Sr.

Author of, *Rich Shepherd, Poor Sheep.*

Pastor of Bethel Church, Richmond Heights, FL

Table of Contents

INTRODUCTION

Invitation: an act of inviting, a request (spoken or written) to participate or be present or take part in something, attraction or incentive, allurement.

Many times, in life, we are presented with an invitation of some kind; an invitation to attend an event, or an invitation into someone's personal space. Without an invitation into someone's space, you are considered an unwelcomed visitor.

An invitation is a mutual agreement between the person who invites and the person who accepts the invitation. Otherwise, it can be said, "They crashed the party."

We live in an era where there is an over-saturation of sex! We are surrounded by and our space is invaded with sexual immorality. We have surrendered sexual purity and most in society seems content with abusing God's good gift. Much of this is a result of our space and body being violated. God created us in His perfect image, however, Satan tempts us with sexual immorality to dehumanize and distract men and women, causing them to forget or to deny their Creator.

RAPE: any person causes another person of any age to engage in a sexual act by...

1. Using force against that other person

2. Causing grievous bodily harm to any person

3. Threatening or placing that other person in fear that any person will be subjected to death grievous bodily harm, or kidnapping

4. Rendering another person unconscious

5. Administering to another person by force or threat of force or without the

knowledge or permission of that person a drug, intoxicant, or other similar substance and is guilty of rape and shall be punished. Nearly 90,000 people reported being raped in the US in 2008, there is an arrest rate of 25%, the US Bureau of statistics states 91% of rape victims are female and 9% male, 99% of rapist are male.

Oftentimes, when people hear of molestation or sexual immorality, it is hastily assumed you are talking about penetration. Although penetration can be a major component, sometimes a sexual violation can come from a touch or a word that is impure. As a child, I recall how dirty I felt when someone touched me inappropriately. In addition, I recall the impure, insidious words that were spoken which made my stomach quiver. I desire to shine a light to this secret sin, of rape and molestation, which opens the door for so much more; in order to be made whole in your present, you must deal with your past!

This book will discuss someone who had their life altered because of a "Non-presented Invitation" from a person who invaded their space and never asked for permission; and most importantly, was never given a right to come in.

PART I

"You stole my innocence you stole my light and now all I do is cry all night, and ask the question, 'Why is this my fight' I opened my mouth and cried for help, but nothing came out, oh I am in hell. My voice was stolen and now there is doubt, Oh, can you heal me of all this pain, and God says this is for my gain, I carried you through the trial and the pain, so I can have kingdom gain; there are so many people that need your story, so go get healed and give him all the glory"

Written By Annaliza

I am writing this book to tell my story of how I overcame sexual abuse of many forms. Hopefully, it will help you see yourself through the mirror of my testimony. I have been talked to inappropriately, I have been touched inappropriately as a child and as a teenager, yet a lot of the things I endured happen in my college/adult life; however, it didn't stop there!

During times of inappropriate interactions with the opposite sex, seeds of fear and being scared to open my mouth and speak against the things that was done to me. Because the seed was planted in my youth, you grow up and it's as if you are reliving this thing all over again.

In the NSVRC, national sexual violence resource center, statistic states more than 1/3 of women who report being raped before age 18, will also experience rape as an adult. I was no different! In my adulthood, I was taken advantage of and I said nothing because, in my mind I felt like because I was out drinking/partying, that I opened myself to being violated. Not saying I deserved it, but I was there, and vulnerable. The aforementioned is the thinking pattern of most victims. We take on the blame, shame, and the embarrassment instead of going out and telling someone so we can receive help.

Instead we live with the trauma and act out what we are feeling in other ways. Sometimes we open doors in our lives trying to mask the pain we feel, no matter how hard we try to move forward and put the event out of our mind. (It never seem to go away) Instead we relive the pain that opened the door of reality for us, "that there are people in this world who're corrupt/heartless and not what they seem to be. It also uncovers the deception in our nation while unveiling the bitter truth that we must deal with in life. I remember going out with a girlfriend and after the party instead of taking me home, she took me to her house, and she proceeded to take off my clothes and performed oral sex on me. I remember engaging in the act, but I thought I had no choice!

But that devil is a liar!!! You have a choice if you can muster up enough courage, strength to say, "No", but the real power comes when you expose the person for who they are.

When you are abused as a child, we tend to mimic what we see and duplicate the behavior. We truly need to get help before it becomes a real problem, but as an adult if you violate someone against their wishes you need to pay dearly for your actions. Let's talk about this as well; if you are out here lying on people saying someone touched you and they did not, you deserve to get the same punishment, sentence as the person you lied on.

These things we don't want to talk about. I believe, I was always a target for people trying to touch, molest or take advantage of me against my wishes because of the way I looked. God protected me for a longtime, there have been situations that I had to fight my way out of. I have been through a lot (like Marvin Sapp song say I don't look like what I been through), nevertheless God has always kept me.

By having that relationship with God, He brought healing to me. I am also writing this book so you can 1) know the signs, 2) know that you don't have to go through this alone, 3) know that God can heal every wound, scar. Freedom comes when you deal with the issue and don't allow the issue to take over your life. You need to know why you are the way you are; and then change it. The power to change the course of your destiny lies in your hands, God will never go against your will to remain the same.

I want you to wake up and take your life back, so it does not happen to your children, or family member, or a friend. The Bible says to owe no man nothing but to love them. If you have been raped or someone violated you against your wishes, it's time to speak up against our abusers. It must stop with you.

When your voice is stolen? And someone invaded your space, it creates so much scarring, that honestly only God can heal.

Some people experience Post Traumatic Stress Disorder (PTSD). It can make you scared of saying, "No" to the invitation of someone's advance. It can bring about a hatred for that particular sex of the person who abused and violated you. Yet I am writing this book just to say just because those things happen to you, you don't have to allow it to dictate or ruin your life, freedom is yours, but you must acknowledge what was done is not your fault. You are fearfully and wonderfully made; God made you in his image and you are beautiful, you are loved. God made no mistake when he created you, his love for you is never ending. No matter what we do; nothing can separate you from his love!

The person that violated me against my wishes when I was intoxicated, when I was scared, or when I wasn't in my right mind at the time, they are the ones that did this act on their own.

I didn't want it, I didn't initiate it, I didn't deserve it, and I didn't lead them on to believe I wanted it. Dysfunctional people do things sometimes because of learned behavior or they are acting out what was done to them, or they have power struggle and or control issues! They feel stronger when they make you feel weak.

Whatever their sick reason for doing what they do, it's time to expose people for what they do. Then and only then they can go get help or go to jail where they will have time to think about their actions and what they have done and seek healing. There has been no repercussion for their actions that's why they go on to do the very same thing to someone else over and over again.

Awareness is the key to healing and deliverance. I want to make sure to bring awareness to this epidemic of taking control of someone's body against their wishes. By using my own experience to showcase things that might be going on in your own life, that we tend not to look at as abuse, or if you do look at it as abuse or rape, you ignore it in fear of what might happen if I speak out against it. The reason I used saying,

"No" to the invitation was because you don't have to accept anybody's invitation if you don't want to, and if you didn't get an invitation, and you crash someone's party, you have the power to call the police and get them tossed out of the party or if they don't comply then they get taken to jail.

When someone violates you or take advantage of you sexually against your will, it's illegal and they should be reported to the authorities. I believe this is the reason so many people keep repeating the same crime! They know we are going to keep quiet (because this is what a lot of victims were taught) especially when it's someone we know, but your freedom is at stake if you shut up and do nothing.

If we would just call out these predators, they would think twice about the repercussion of violating someone else against their wishes. These predators are getting off scotch free and going on to do the very same thing to someone else! Especially within the family. If Uncle John or the family friend molested or raped you, it won't stop there, he/she will keep coming after you, your cousin, or your sister/brother. In this day we live in, they are not only attacking the girls they are now attacking the boys as well.

This is my story I pray that reading this book you will get the courage to speak out against your abuser or go get help by talking to someone and releasing the anxiety, fear, shame, secret from consuming your life. God is a healer, so I hope you have a relationship with him because he can truly lead you in what to do. My journey has been a testimony for others to know that you are not the only person it has happened to, you are not alone, and you don't have to go through this alone and in silence!

According to the National Sexual Violence Resource Center statistic (NSVRC)...

- 1 in 5 women and 1 in 7 men will be raped at some point in their lives

- In the us 1 in 3 women and 2 in 6 men experience some form of contact sexual violence in their lifetime

- 51.1% of female victims of rape reported being raped by intimate partners and 40.8% by an acquaintance

- 52.4% of male victims report being raped by an acquaintance and

52.1% by a stranger

- 91% of victims of rape and sexual assault are females and 9% are male

- 8 out of 10 cases of rape the victim knew the perpetrator

Child Sexual Abuse

- 1 in 4 girls and 1 in 6 boys will be sexually abused before they turn 18 years old

- 30% of women were between 10-17 or younger at the time of their 1st completed rape victimization

- 96% of people who sexually abuse children are male and 76.8% of people who sexually abuse children are adults

- 34% of people who sexually abuse children are family member of the child

- 90% of sexual assault victims on college campuses do not report the assault

- 20-25% of college women and 15% of men were victims or forced sex during their time in college

Rape is the most under reported crime!

My story began as a young girl growing up with both my parents in the home. My mother was a stay at home mother and my father was very strict in my childhood due to his Chinese culture.

At a very young age I was taught the principles of waiting until you were married to be sexual; but also, at a very young age, I had friends of the family and family members of the opposite sex who invited themselves to say and do inappropriate things against my wishes. It was a contravention! I was so innocent and naive to the point I would not tell anyone. Like so many other victims, I held it in but internally I was deeply devastated wondering why this happened to me.

I grew up in a family of people who had their own dysfunction. My mother was a homemaker and she was an anointed woman, she was a prophetic intercessor and dreamer. She was very passive to life's challenges, but she was a warrior in the spirit. My father on the other hand was very strong, confident and strict. I grew up in a home where I never saw the display of affection or love. In Chinese culture they do not believe in public display of affection. And I grew up thinking that love was spoken and not shown.

Many years ago, while on a journey to deal with my past and discover who I was, God began to unveil things that I had hidden away in my mind that I chose not to deal with. While on this journey, God said to me that He would take me back and show me the things that I chose to forget. This was when God began to give me an understanding of how the cycle of sexual and emotional abuse began. If someone took advantage of you and took something so precious and you were never given the opportunity to say, "No" this could later become a thorn in your life's journey.

Most people don't understand that physical and emotional abuse can be heartbreaking for a child! Fear and anxiety will overtake them, and they become defenseless, not knowing what to do or what to say. It creates insecurities and sometime lack of confidence. There are children committing suicide at an alarming rate because of being bullied and or sexual assault.

Parents take this as a warning and pay attention to signs of abuse. By doing this, you can save your child's life from great pain and despair. All my life, I remember hearing a song on the radio and it made me feel so dirty and filthy on the inside. I would quickly turn it off. I never understood why until God revealed to me that when I was molested, that very song was playing on the radio. At that moment everything flooded back to my memory and it all made sense; that song was a trigger point for me.

I wanted to write this book to help people that have been sexually violated identify if they have been victimized. If you ever experienced someone's crude or inappropriate words, someone showed you inappropriate pictures, someone touched you in private places, or they exposed themselves to you without your permission...you may be a victim of sexual abuse.

People don't understand that a word spoken inappropriately can be as damaging as the physical act of rape! For years I kept hearing those sharp and evil words spoken to me about how they were going to take my virginity. "You little Chinese/Jamaican so and so, I'm going to get you!" That thing disturbed me for years! The same can be said about that inappropriate touch that I was forced to experience. It disgusted me so much that this nasty old man would touch me in such a way that was so vile to me (he only touched my leg, but it was inappropriate and disturbing to me). I felt so defenseless not knowing what to do or say, but God said, "It's time to take back your voice because when you are violated your voice is silenced."

Many times, attorneys in rape cases ask the victim did you scream, or did you say no, but if you have never been put in a situation like that you would never understand. Your voice is totally taken from you, sometimes you feel inside of yourself that you are screaming stop, but the words never come out because of the shock of what is happening. It is a terrifying ordeal, especially when you are a child and don't know what to do and have no strength or power to fight off this vile person that is violating you. It's sad that children are now dealing with adult circumstances and situation that they shouldn't have to.

I look at the world we live in and there are so many people confused about their sexuality, and a lot of the confusion is due to someone close (be it family or friend, male or female) coming into your space without invitation. There are homosexuals that were violated by someone of the same sex and now they are battling with their identity because they don't know if they are heterosexual or homosexual. A female friend of mine once told me about her female cousin who molested her and for my friend's entire life, she has walked around fighting a spirit of homosexuality. That defensive thought would pop in her head and she would be fighting to stay normal. It becomes a struggle in your mind because every thought you are battling is am I a homosexual or am I a heterosexual. (Whatever your preference that's your choice but as a Christian I honor the word of God that speaks about procreation with a man and a woman). That's where you must choose to cast down every imagination. That person of the same sex released a spirit of immorality that leaves you confused about what you like or dislike. Like so many young people who are curious about sex and they open the door to that spirit by experimenting with men and women.

I truly believe that as parents we need to be very careful about who we allow around our children, and even though many of us tell our children to come and talk to us if someone touches them inappropriately, as a child you are so violated and depending on what that person said to you, you are so fearful that you keep quiet. As a child how would you feel? If an adult cannot deal with this situation, how can we expect a child to handle such paralyzing ordeal? Their mind and intellect cannot fathom what is going on much less to articulate what they feel or what was done to them.

Even at an older age, you feel the same way, wondering if it's your fault or thinking of ways that you could have avoided the intrusion, but there is nothing that can be done if someone invites themselves without your invitation. Sometimes it is people that you once trusted, and you are so devastated that this happened to you, not knowing what to do or how to respond sometimes you will still be around the violator and never discuss it. You both pretend as if it never happened.

As an adult, I was working at a job in Miami where one of my supervisors would leave me lude notes on my desk asking what color panties I had on, and then he took it to another level and while working together on a project one evening he came behind me and said turn around and when I did their he was exposing himself to me and that thing disturbed me. I still remember how I felt, and how it chipped away a piece of me. I tried to take my voice back by informing management, but nothing was done. As a result, because of the inaction of management, I felt violated again because I was left to rehash the event without vindication.

In addition, I recall an incident on my birthday where I went out with friends and they bought me some champagne. After having a glass of champagne, and me not being an alcohol drinker, after I took several sips, I was so intoxicated that I truly couldn't remember going to a hotel room where both my close friends took advantage of me. I didn't remember the actual act until the alcohol I drank that night wore off.

I tried to put this out of my mind like it never happened, then I started to blame myself (oh I asked for this or I didn't stop it, or I shouldn't have gone out etc.). You may have participated being out of control and making them feel validated that you wanted it. However, I wondered, "How could I give consent, if I was drunk?" Here your voice is taken; someone invited themselves into your space and never asked if you were okay, you were never given the choice to say, "Yes" or "No." Therefore, going forward in life, you may feel that when you are in similar situations that you don't have a right to say, "No."

Saying, "No" to the invitation takes courage and God's strength; until you are in a place of wholeness from your past, you will continue to fall prey to the same cycles. If you don't trust yourself to be alone, then go with a group of people, or don't go any place that is questionable by yourself. But here is the key, make sure you take people you can trust, and more importantly make sure you take God with you.

I recently heard about a young lady that was physically attractive and had many associates disguising themselves as friends, but were secretly jealous and envious of her beauty, one night they put her in a situation where these jealous women she called friends allowed someone to put a mickey in her drink, then left her alone to be violated. They considered that a prank. Make sure that you know those that hang around you. You can't trust everyone to have your back in a situation where you are vulnerable and unable to stand up for yourself. Getting turned up to the point of not being coherent and aware of what's going on is a risk that can be very costly. I too have been young and remember wanting to fit in and have fun, yet we need to be aware at all times.

You must be careful with the people you invite into your space. If you are around someone that is dealing with open sin in their life, you can find yourself enticed by that spirit. This is another reason why you need to be very careful of the people who are doing your hair, hands, and feet; these are entry points on your body that will allow access to negative spirits into your life.

I am reminded of a story in the Bible where this king's son wanted Tamar so badly that he crashed into her space without invitation or warning. Not only was she violated but he turned around and hated her for something he did...and to top it off, she was promised to another man. In those days, victims were told to keep abuse silent, so after the rape, Tamar remained desolate in her brother's house, her voice taken, gripped in shame and trauma from the abuse she suffered at the hands of her half-brother.

Often, people are violated by predators that are family and or friends! They still must see these people and be in their sphere; every time you see them it is just a reminder of what happened. Therefore, so many times it becomes repetitious; if the perpetrator got away with it before, it makes them think they can continue and there will be no consequences for their actions. They truly are predators that prey on those they feel have no voice or they have no one to turn to that they can share this trauma with. I believe it gives them some sick satisfaction of getting away with it once again. In some instances, it's common knowledge that a predator has violated other people in the family too. If someone had stepped up and confronted this person and made it known what he or she did, maybe others could have been protected.

I got married young so that protected me from so much, but I know many people who were single and very promiscuous and when asked why they were that way, most answered that they didn't know. As I dug further, I found out that they too were molested at some point in life. You may be in a family where there is a repetitive cycle of sexual abuse. It happened to the parent and they don't know how to have a voice for you because they have yet to find their own voice. You can't protect someone when you cannot protect yourself. I endured abuse and kept silent because I watched my mother endure so much and she never said a word. I thought that was what you were supposed to do, stay silent to keep the peace...What peace...when yours was violently taken from you!

For the longest time, I tried to erase everything out of my mind that had happened to me, but I found out if you don't deal with it now, it will take over your life later. It changed the way I viewed men and it influenced the way I responded to the opposite sex. I was a runner and truly tried to stay out of situations that I knew I couldn't control. I didn't trust myself with men, so I avoided them at all costs. I did not date or go anywhere alone with the opposite sex. On the other hand, there were many people, who instead of being a runner like me, would have these Relationships' or they would go on these dates and say, "Yes" to something that they had every intention of saying, "No" to. Many people can sense insecurity and use it to their advantage. They know where you are weak, and their motive is to play on your frailty while making sure you fall.

All my life I desired to wait until my wedding night before I engaged in sexual intercourse because I was told that this was the best gift you could give to your husband. Although I wound up marrying the person that I lost my virginity to, it was not my choice to be intimate before marriage. Once again, I was overcome by the dysfunction of not knowing how to say, "No." Don't get me wrong, I wasn't forced or coerced, but being in a situation where the other party does not know that you are battling with wounds that stem so deep and you truly didn't know that you had a voice to say those two little letters: NO.

I had a family member that violated me as a child and as an adult.

I didn't know how to handle or deal with what was done to me as a child and as an adult, we went out one night to get my mind clear of something I was facing. I didn't see the trap that was set for me! I had a drink that I should have passed on. That drink took me over the top Again, I am not a drinker, but I always felt he did something else to the alcohol. I don't remember leaving the club and neither do I remember him dropping me off at home. When I sobered up, I felt violated and I remembered him doing to me what no family member should be doing; He was on top of me having sex with me! I remember going into a place of depression behind that night and I remember hating to be called beautiful or pretty. I thought it was a curse for men to always and consistently desire me. I remember wishing I was ugly so men would leave me alone. I hated the attention but come to find out that no matter how you look, your shape or size it doesn't change the narrative. After this, I went into a place where I firmly believe that if I did not have a relationship with God, I would have lost my mind.

In the body of Christ, we don't talk about these things because we feel that we can do deliverance and pray, and it simply goes away. However, this thing must be discussed to really get to the source of the behavior of the perpetrator and change the behavior of the violated. People are not sexually immoral without a reason! A lot of times the predators themselves either have been molested and they become the molester, or they have been molested and they remain the victim all their lives. Understand this, "We can get our voices back!" As hard as it may seem, we can start by talking to someone you can trust and tell them what happened. If needed, seek professional counseling because it can also help people as well.

I had to kill the effects of the emotional and sexual trauma I experienced. I made a vow that I had to kill that thing in me to protect my seed in the future from going through what I went through. I was very transparent with my children and I made sure to never put them in a predicament that would allow a predator to prey on them. I am not saying I was always suspicious or fearful, but I made sure to never put them in a place where I could not protect them. I got delivered and gave them over to God. I trusted Him with my children because He promised to keep and protect them from every snare and trap set against them. If you don't let go, you will become enslaved to your fear.

For many years, people were only concerned about their daughters being molested or raped but you must watch over your boys because it can certainly happen to them as well. As parents, we have to be able to communicate with our children and discern their actions. If your child doesn't want to go over a family/friend house, you need to ask why. You must have a relationship with your children where they feel they can talk to you without judgment, and you should listen to hear what they are not telling you. When they tell you something, you need to be like the knight in shining armor and validate them. I think a lot of times it hurts more when they come to you and nothing is done. Or worse, they feel they are not believed. That is devastating having to deal with what happened to them and to add insult to injury, you don't believe them.

Most likely, people are the way they are because of a learned behavior. Sometimes it's hereditary or it can truly be a bloodline curse. Yes, some things have been passed down from generation to generation.

The spirit of lust takes on many forms. You can be promiscuous, but sex can be repulsive to you. You can be unsure about your identity and not know if you are gay or straight, love masturbation and/or porn, incest runs in your bloodline, or there are even some people that love the strip clubs or even prostitutes, but do not know why! It could be a generational or bloodline curse in operation.

As parents, we must be very careful which doors we open because they eventually come after your seed. Remember the sins of the father fall on the children. Sometimes we see children acting in inappropriate ways and are shocked wondering where they could have gotten that behavior from. Look at yourself, what are you doing behind closed doors? Children often mimic what they see or act out what has been done to them. Pay very close attention to their behaviors. As a child, I found myself humping on another child because of what had been done to me and as I grew up; that thing haunted me, but I did not know any better.

If you are a single parent that allows all kinds of men/women into your house, your child might see that as being okay and grow up and mimic that learned behavior. God forbid, if these men/women that you allow into your home turn out to be the very predators that I am talking about. Sometimes it might not be penetration, but they say things to your child that plays in their head and plants seeds that eventually grow into something they never intended. Or, it's a touch that scars them for life. If not dealt with, these things can come back to haunt their life. Abusers were likely once abused at some point in their life. Quite commonly, they will either abuse others or wind up abusing themselves.

The question to ask is, "How do we get to the other side of abuse?"

The short answer is, "By allowing God to come into our heart and take control!" He will show you what to confront and what not to confront. In addition, He will protect you when no one else can. God will begin to walk you through moments that most would choose to erase from their memory. He will gently bring things back to your memory that you blocked out of your thoughts.

For the men that was raped by their babysitter or an older woman. And now a spirit of perversion is loosed upon you. And so many men are running around here, having sex with every woman possible. They too were hurt and taken advantage of by predators, but many men talk little about it because the old boy's tale. It's ok for a boy to get taken advantage of because it makes you a man, so they claim. No rape is rape!

Therefore, you have some men angry at women for what was done to them or angry about what they saw around other men and women, (remember your relationship with your parents will ultimately influence your relationship with others). So now they are running around hurting women because they are hurt because of what was done to them. They hate women therefore they are living a homosexual lifestyle because the other gender disappointed them. And the fact that men are so silent and taught to be strong and deal with things without expressing their feelings. They never seek help. They never get the help. They never seek to be healed, but it's time for us all to be made whole. Seeking help is imperative to your healing!

It's not ok for you as a man to live a life void of understanding or to walk around dysfunctional and calling it what man do.

Personally, I relied on God to walk me through that valley of the shadow of death and now I will fear no evil because I know He is with me. His rod and his staff comforted me, and He prepared a table before me in the presence of my enemy. He also anointed my head with oil until my cup ran over. Surely goodness and mercy follow me, all the days of my life and I will dwell in the house of the Lord forever!

I can testify to you that God is truly a keeper. I know it is deeper for those who have been raped. Not only do you need God, but you need to talk to someone that can listen to bring closure to the traumatic and gripping abuse you faced. You are not to blame! We are often left to feel that the abuse was our fault but that is not true, these people are sick and truly need to get help.

There are many places that we are invited to that we truly need to say, "No" to the invitation. This is a major reason why it is so important to ask God for permission. And allow him to order your steps daily.

The scripture says,

"Acknowledge Him in all thy ways
and He will direct your paths."

Proverbs 3:6 (KJV)

Therefore, ask God for yourself and your children, "Can I go Lord? Is it okay for me to release my kids in the care of others?"

This all started with Eve being seduced by the enemy and not being able to say, "No" to the invitation. The serpent offered her to bite the fruit to receive all the awesome things that would happen to her. The door opened when Adam was told to watch over his wife, and he took his eyes off her and allowed the enemy to beguile his wife.

We open things in our lives, and the lives of our children/family, when we invite the wrong people into our home/space, watch the wrong things, or speak the wrong things, and when we allow the wrong people to touch or lay hands on us just to name a few.

Another example was the prophet that received an invitation to dinner. Even though he got specific instruction from the Lord to not stop until his assignment was completed, he decided to disobey the instructions God gave him. The old prophet invited him to dinner and was able to deceive him and cause him to be destroyed by the lion. Had he said, "No" to the invitation he would have fulfilled God's plan for him and probably would have lived.

In Proverbs 23, we have this selfish man and the ruler inviting him to dinner, you know who he is and still, you accept his invitation. Just because he invited you doesn't mean he is not the person you know him to be. His motive and intentions are not pure; this invitation will cost much more than the dinner itself.

All three scenarios are examples of invitations that should have been ignored; look at the fruit and if it doesn't bear witness with your spirit then you know not to entertain it. So many times, we have a gut feeling that something is not right, yet we discard it. Then later, when you investigate or talk to someone that was raped by someone they knew, they would often say, "I knew something wasn't right, or it didn't feel right, or you saw something you just couldn't put your finger on about a person." Follow the discernment of the Holy Spirit or the inclination that you feel. Follow the alarms and the red flags (means stop!!!) people give us. They are there for you to stop and assess everything.

As a result of what I have endured, growing up I was a very quiet introvert. Who minded her own business and kept to myself.

Later in life, I got to the point that I got tired of the abuse and I became very angry because I felt there was no one there to protect me, nor understand what I was going through. I went from being this very nice person to a mean individual because that was the only way I felt I could protect myself. I would cut you up with words and you would walk away before realizing you had been cut. I was very skilled with my tongue (funny how skilled I was at cutting people, but not skilled enough to tell the invaders no).

Being mean was my defense mechanism. When a guy tried to talk to me before he could get close, I had already sized him up and knew by a minute into the conversation what he was about; and I would shut him down completely. I didn't want anyone to get close to me. If you showed me any negative signs at all, I would shut you out and I didn't care. I had to protect myself from being used or violated ever again. I was skilled at discerning the red flags, yet unable to stand up for myself and say no to the invitation.

I remember my apostle telling me I was very intimidating to men. After looking at myself after that I was very shocked by what I saw. I never wanted to be hurt or betrayed again so I would look at a man and tell him "No" before he could even get the chance to say anything to me. As the saying goes, "Hurt people, hurt people." Oh yes, I hurt people as well. Because of years of disappointment and betrayal I experienced, I wouldn't allow anyone to get close because I truly felt I could not trust anyone. I was quick to cut people off when they made a mistake. I got others before they had a chance to get me.

I fought for my deliverance and I fought for my voice. No one knew what I was going through.

Going into my first marriage, when things got trying in our marriage, I resorted to being mean and didn't know how to express what I was feeling to my husband. It's like sitting there waiting for them to mess up and prove that no one is to be trusted. Unknowingly, we self-sabotage relationships to protect ourselves from being let down. You must constantly fight to stay free! Even though my ex-husband was my best friend and we had an amazing relationship the first 8 years of our 13 years of marriage. Hurt people hurt people.

I thought I was totally healed years after my divorce and then I got with someone that had his own issues that he was not healed from, now we are intimate. Guess what? That spirit can be transferred if you are not careful. So here I walked through deliverance to have this thing coming at me in other forms. That's why you need to wait on your spouse and when he finds you, or you find her, make sure they have been delivered from their issues. Thank God I had a relationship with the Lord, and I am one that stays in prayer, so God was able to show me what was going on and I was able to discern things that this person never shared and understanding what he was not saying when he tried to explain.

Saying "No" to the invitation spilled over into relationships where I knew they were not for me, but because of the paralysis of not being able to voice how I really felt, I entered the 2nd marriage that I knew was wrong. I allowed his emergency to be mine, I remember God downloading everything about this person and told me not to continue on in the relationship, yet I disobeyed God. On our wedding day everything came to stop us from getting married, yet with all the red flags I didn't know how to say "NO" I remember telling my second husband about my abuse and every time we got into an argument about his behavior with his female friends, he would find a way of throwing it in my face. Now even though he is not the person that violated me, he is the person that knows and chooses to hold me responsible for what I shared with him in secret, instead he became the enemy as well.

We think that if we get married the problems will all go away, but if you've never sought counseling or allowed God to heal you, your spouse will wind up paying for your mistrust and wounds. Reasonably because your spouse will trigger things in you that you haven't dealt with or been healed from.

In one relationship my friend had no clue what I had been through and this was one of the reasons why the relationship didn't work. Even though I had a great relationship with him, I was rather controlling, and wanted to ensure that no one took advantage of me. I was very strong in my conviction. I wasn't willing to bend and meet him half way. I ran away from the relationship because it really required me to address my issues and allow him in. It ended because it was easier to walk away. With another relationship even though I was healed he was not, so here we go! Not knowing how to say "No" to the invitation will cause you to accept relationships that should have never been. If there are insecurities you will entertain the person that feeds into that place, just as if you are weak you want someone that is strong, or if you feel no one stuck up for you in the past you pick someone that you feel will defend/fight for you. If you do not get healed you may pick someone to appease the dysfunctional side of you, only to later realize this person is truly not who God wanted for you, or what you would want for yourself. In dysfunction, one may choose dysfunction. On the other hand, if one is healed, they'll choose a healed person. We tend to attract who we really are internally. It's possible to choose right, after you have chosen wrong.

PART 2

"You came and took a piece of me and now I struggle with my identity. I wonder all day and night, if this is truly my fight, so I give it to you Lord and lay it down, because no more will I frown on the things that came to steal kill and destroy me, because you my Lord kept me. So now I can hold my head up high and know that I no longer have to lie about the pain I felt in my struggle for freedom. I now know that I know who I am and what I want, and no longer can the devil taunt Me and make me question my sexuality, because of my God, I am free!"

Written by Annaliza

When you have been molested or raped, it opens doors while releasing a spirit of perversion and lust. And now you have desires and sensations that have to be filled and some people begin self-gratification to feed that urge and that's where masturbation, promiscuity, homosexuality, and other sexual habits enter. Some people resort to celibacy to abstain from sex all together because of what happened to them, I promote celibacy until you are married and whole. Because women if you are having sex with multiple partners, remember men deposit and women receive, so you are inviting the spirit of everyone they slept with in your spirit. So until you become healed and made whole refrain from being intimate. Remain celibate until your mate comes. There are some men and women who cannot have an orgasm with their spouse because of years of satisfying themselves. Consequently, masturbation is the only way they can have an orgasm. The Devil!

Finding out the root cause to this behavior is a major key to breakthrough. It is so disheartening to know that you have a spouse that don't arouse you, or satisfy your urge, because of previous abuse. You cannot be intimate with your spouse because of the lack of being satisfied by them to the point of you needing to be self- gratified. Please seek to get help! I had another friend who shared that as a teenager every time her mother would leave her home alone, she found comfort in touching herself, so whenever she needed comfort she resorted to masturbation. Please understand that every behavior has a root. If you were molested and they performed oral sex on you and that is all you want because you think that is it. There are so many dysfunctions that stem from you being violated.

I knew the patterns and the way people act when they have been molested, remember I said it can be a word, a touch, or worst of all penetration.

I had a friend who would always keep women around him...all the time! I asked, "What is that about?" I asked because he thought it was normal. I knew it stemmed from a dysfunctional place, but I did not know the root. Come to find out, quite frequently, a family member would tell him he was gay. To prove he was not gay, he always became very promiscuous and had to have many female friends, even at the cost of losing his marriage.

He couldn't let go of what kept him being the man they said he wasn't. From a word! Life and death are in the power of the tongue. Words can last longer than any scar! We don't invite spirits into our life but there are doors that we open in our lives, or our parents have opened. We must look at patterns and see where they truly come from. If you dig deep enough you will find out that a lot of dysfunctions came from somebody not saying, "No" to the invitation. I had another friend where it was the opposite; she had to have men around. A woman let her down, so now she felt if she keeps men around, she will feel protected and safe. She would always defend them no matter what and it dawned on me one day that the abuse from her mother made her feel she could not trust another woman. Therefore, she leaned on the men and trusted them even if they were no good.

I know there is freedom in the testimonies of others because, the Word of God says,

> *"...They overcome him by the blood of the Lamb and by the words of our testimony..."*

Revelation 12:10 (KJV)

Prayerfully, you too can be set free by hearing what I've been through. From the thoughts that used to consume me...

"Shall I live, or shall I die at the innocence stolen by this guy. You never were invited to come on in. Not even was I warned of your blatant sin. Oh, I cried, and I scream yet you stole my voice to fight and to say I have no choice, of saying yes or no. To no avail, you forced your way in. How I wished my senses were keen enough back then. Every time I think of that day it leaves me with so much to say. I will never forget what you did. Vile and disgusting are you to me, and I have to acknowledge and deal with what you did. Taking back my joy and peace stolen from me all the time I blamed myself. I resorted to talking to no one about what you did, shut down, and ended up trusting no one. Only to get to this day now I can see that I am free..."

Written by Annaliza

There are times, where in order to heal, you need to tell the accused what they did to you. For me, God allowed me to pray for them and I was able to forgive them without telling them to their faces. For others, I know you need to look them in the face and get an answer, and sometimes we want an apology; but even if you never get one, in order to move forward you must learn to forgive. It's a challenge to forgive, we tend to choose to harbor the resentment and never want to forgive them because you feel they don't deserve to be forgiven. I know you have heard the saying, forgiving them is not for them but for you. Forgiveness frees you and brings you to a place of peace. Many times, we harbor unforgiveness and it festers into anger and bitterness that can later potentially produce cancer and other sickness and disease. The Bible refers to bitterness as wormwood, which can be equivalent to cancer. Therefore, we must at all cost forgive! If you want your heavenly father to forgive you of your sins; you must do the same for others who have done you wrong. If you cannot physically confront that person there are other ways to get answers and closure. I remember writing a letter to the accused and putting everything I ever wanted to tell them about what they did, in that letter. This method might not work for you, yet it brought a lot of healing to me, but everything we go through on this journey is a process. Years later, one of the accused passed away, and because he was a friend of the family, my mother asked me if I was going to the funeral I remember how I snapped. This person has passed away and I was still harboring resentment for him being a disgusting old man. Who in a subtle way was chipping away at me little by little by the things he did. Thank God he never got a chance to complete his assignment against my life.

When God begins to walk us through the process of healing, and He begins to show us things and makes us confront our fears, yield to it because our Father in heaven knows best. He knows when you are strong enough to face those fears. Sometimes we try to force it, but the process will take God to walk you through deliverance and freedom from any violation that came to grip your life. If other attempts at healing fail, you may need to seek professional, help to gain emotional stability.

You would be shocked about how common it is for someone male or female to be molested by someone they know and may be close to. It's time for people to speak out about the dysfunction and shame the devil because when we stay silent, we give the enemy room to continue to play on that fear and cause you to live life in fear and bondage.

I know God brought me through this journey, so you too can be set free because it truly affects every area of your life. It steals your voice in every area where you should speak up; you don't speak in fear of disappointing, fear of shame, fear of what people will think about you, or just plain fear and intimidation.

The Bible says,

"For God hath not given you the spirit of fear, but of power, love and a sound mind."

2 Timothy 1:7 (KJV)

But the enemy comes to invade your mind by plaguing you with the memory of what happened. The Word says as a man thinketh so is he; that's why the Bible talks about; man commits adultery the moment he thinks a thing in his heart; he sins from the thought. That's why we are to cast down every imagination and every high thing that 'exalteth' itself against the knowledge of God and bringing it into captivity to the obedience of Christ.

We now see the epidemic where people are coming forth after years or decades of being a victim of rape, and when the accused is finally punished the victims cry and feel so justified and free. Remember, this thing never goes away unless you allow God to heal those broken places. God is truly able to keep you from falling and present you faultless before the King. God can heal those broken places, and true healing can begin when you address and acknowledge that there is a problem.

Once you have addressed that there is an issue, now seek help; professional help. You need to seek counseling and talk about what happened in order to get deliverance, and true healing. We think "I'm not crazy, I don't need to see anyone," I know sometimes in the African American community, it is frowned upon to seek counseling, but I am telling you some cases are so severe that you really need to seek professional help. My case might be different from yours. God took me through my journey and brought to my memory everything I tried to block and made me deal with it like I stated before I had to fight for my freedom. No one knows you better than you, and God knows you best.

I had a friend that was convinced she had lesbian thoughts because of being molested by a family member of the same sex. When she would think things or even look at the opposite sex in a way that she felt was not right; I would tell her to just pray about it and let it go, I thought she was being dramatic and it wasn't that deep. She thought if she could continue to get deliverance then it would go away, but sometimes if you have prayed and gone through the deliverance line over and over and nothing happens, it's time to go a step further and seek help. No one know what you are going through but you.

You must fight against that thing because the enemy says one thing, but you must release the Word of God and tear down every imagination. The enemy knows what your struggle is; he knows if you have a weakness for sex/drugs/alcohol/lying etc., so whatever your weakness is he is always going to plague you with that. Once again, cast down every imagination and every high thing that exalts itself against the knowledge of God and bring it into captivity to the obedience of God.

Just because you've been healed and delivered from something doesn't mean you stop fighting to stay healed and delivered. The enemy doesn't fight fair! Just because you are whole in that area don't stop him from trying to bring you back to that place. I have heard people say that if you have been delivered for real you don't have to worry about it anymore; I don't believe that to be true. An alcoholic need to stay away from alcohol, just as a drug addict needs to stay away from drugs.

You need to continue to protect yourself until you get to a place where the enemy knows he cannot tempt you with that thing anymore. Then, and only then, will he stop and move on to something else. Remember the enemy come to steal, kill and destroy.

PART 3

"Say no to the invitation, how you were not invited but you came on in and violated and stole my innocence, you took a piece of me and now I come to collect, that piece that was taken and left me feeling empty and confused about my identity and my sexuality, it was devastating and hurtful and I could not see how this gruesome thing happened to me, I cried I screamed, and you didn't stop, now I'm left to deal here on the spot, with what you did and how I feel, I went through the fire and was not burned because my daddy was truly concerned about the hurt and the pain I endured, and now all I want is to be cured, you invited yourself and crashed my life and now all I want is to be a good wife, but the memory of that day taunts my life, and all I can do is fight, fight, fight for my peace, for my freedom and for my joy, I say, "NO" to the invitation at all cost."

Written by Annaliza

There was a time this handsome, well dressed, educated, physically fit, and had a body out of this world gentleman asked me out, and the spirit of the Lord said, "No." He tried so hard and the answer was still no. I remember telling a friend and she was like, girl I would have gone out with him just to get a meal.

Ironically, that's why so many people get caught up in a trap. Don't be desperate for a meal, sex, or companionship but rather use that desperation for God. You can't break bread with everybody, and you can't eat from just anyone; discern and say no. Remember the story of the ruler and the selfish man that was invited to dinner; that invitation can have effects on your life more than that meal is worth. Follow the signs and the inclination you have in your spirit when God says, "No" it's an absolute "No." we must know our worth and stop accepting any and everything. Say "NO" to the invitation that doesn't value and appreciate who God created you to be

I once went to a college party and they were drinking, smoking and doing other things that I chose not to participate in. Before going, I remember that little small voice telling me to stay in the dorm that night, but I chose not to adhere to it, and I went anyway. The party was at an associate's house and I remember having a headache from all the smoking going on, so I went in the back room because they told me to go lie down and take a nap. I woke up to this nasty person on top of me with his clothes off trying to take that which did not belong to him. He was trying to rape me!

He never asked nor received an invitation, at this point I found my voice and said, "No," and I went off. He ran away and avoided me the entire time we were in college. Saying no was good, but still I was dysfunctional because I remained silent and did not tell anyone what had happened to me...another non-invitation. Rape and molestation are at a high rate on college campuses, and let us not even begin with sex trafficking young boys and girls. So, use wisdom and caution on who to trust and when to say no to the invitation. Your parents are not there to protect you so you have to be very sensitive and discerning about who to trust and where you can go. Try to stick with a group and not move around solo on campus. Sometimes predators watch your pattern, movement and behavior and pray on that.

The Word of God says no man can come into your house and strong arm you unless invited to do so; that includes your body as well. If you don't say no and never express the discontent for what they are doing, a person void of understanding and restraint would assume that it's ok to violate you. Too many times the spirit of the Lord warns us, and we still yield to our flesh which can be detrimental to your life. They say one door begets another door; sometimes the doors we open in our lives cause the enemy to come in, now what was a small thing has been blown into something so huge and massive that you truly need help to close the doors.

I have a friend who shared her story of how she lost her virginity because she didn't want to stay at school alone. A friend invited her to go with her off school grounds on lunch to visit with her boyfriend and his friends. The next couple of days she would go over these college guys house with her friend, where they were smoking weed and drinking, unaware the doorway to abuse kept opening wider and wider upon each visit. She began engaging in what they were doing and then one door begat another door, and before she knew it, this college guy was taking this high school girls' virginity. Because she didn't say no to the invitation the doors kept swinging wider and wider. Don't put yourself in compromising situations, where there is no way out. Real friends would never put you in harm's way.

I remember hearing someone say God is not guaranteed to protect you when you are disobedient to him, same with the young prophet who got killed because of his disobedience. Sometimes not following those alarms can cost you your life, or in this case, your virginity. Please be sensitive to what you feel, if something does not feel right go with your gut. If someone doesn't seem right and you see red flags, follow the leading of the holy spirit, say no to the invitation that comes packaged up smelling good, looking good.

It's just discerning those that are around you, there are many times in ministry where people invite themselves into your world by saying they want to help you; but what is your intent and motive, you truly need to seek God and ask him what is the purpose/motive and intent of the person, once again like I stated before don't get to a place where you are suspicious of everybody, but truly getting into the habit of seeking God in everything you do, like the word says in all thy ways acknowledge him and he will direct your path, this is key to success; where it is safety proof and will protect you from danger.

Don't get me wrong some people will go through things in life because God has a plan, some people truly must pick up their cross and follow him. There will be people that will go through some of the same things God had you walk through, so you can identify/empathize with them and tell them how you overcame. We didn't ask for the abuse neither did we invite the dysfunction in our lives; but now that you have walked through the valley of the shadow of death, it's time to fear no evil for God is with you. This was the cross God allowed you to bear, now pick up that cross and follow him to your deliverance. Follow him to a place where he can heal and deliver you. Follow him to that place where your testimony can set someone free.

How about the wife who gets raped by her own husband? I know many might say that this is impossible, but there are times and situations where the wife says no for whatever reason and that man violently forces himself upon his spouse. In her opinion, she was violated. Just because you are married doesn't mean you have the right to take it against the others wish. Since I'm here let's address this issue, I know the Bible says in marriage your body is not your own but belongs to the other, yes! But you respect and love your body, so do the same for your spouse.

For the men and women who deny their spouses, you are truly out of order. I know people who use sex to control and manipulate their spouse, but you are releasing a curse on your house. You should be denying your spouse only to fasting and they must agree with it. I am not talking about being insensitive to your spouse, if he/she is truly sick or not able to compromise, but to deny your husband or wife is a sin.

That's an invitation you need to be saying, "Yes" to. Things from our pasts can cause a lot of mistrust in the marriage chamber when you bring learned behavior taught in the world. The marriage bed is undefiled, so truly allow God to show you how to make love to your spouse; this is an area where we do not allow the Lord in, but this is the very place you need him the most.

Many people that have been molested or raped have issues in the marriage bed; this is where communication needs to take place. Ask the Lord to show you how to please your spouse and bring them to a place of trust and peace with you, or ask your spouse how and where they want to be touched, kissed or caressed, ask them how they want to be made love to. It takes skill from God to undo some things that have been done to us by others. There are so many married couples where a spouse went through the trauma of being molested or raped and goes through the motions of making love without getting any satisfaction. They fake it for your sake; they go through the motions, but they are never satisfied, and sometimes they are so good at faking it you will never know.

Healing begins when you become honest with the person you took a vow with before the Lord. It's a sad thing to go through life faking it and never truly experiencing the ecstasy of an orgasm with your spouse. Be open and honest about what you went through; communicate so that the other person knows and be open to work through it. Tell them how you want to be touched and truly allow God to bring complete joy in the bedroom for both parties.

It's time to speak out and stop holding stuff in because that's what the enemy wants; he would love it if you kept this hidden and never talked about it, so he can continue to taunt you with the thoughts/images of what happened to you. Like they use to say, open your mouth and shame the devil. You truly need to renew your mind after all this and transform your thinking pattern.

The word says to think on those things which are lovely and of good report, think about peace and pursue it; take out the impure thoughts and replace all the negatives with positives. God can do that for you, He truly is a healer and a deliverer. Take the time and really fight for your freedom from those things that came to steal kill and destroy you and close the doors that were opened because of that unwelcomed invitation; give it to God and he will direct your path. Stop the cycle for your seed and stop the cycle for someone else, our silence sometimes allows these predators to continually and repeatedly violate others. If you can't be strong by yourself, tell someone you can trust to stand by your side.

I pray that as you read this book the Holy Spirit will bring to memory the things you suppressed and choose not to deal with. I hope being honest with yourself about what you have faced in your life will bring forth true deliverance to you. You have a right and a choice to say yes or no, and no one has the power or authority over your body to make an invitation where you have no voice to say yes or no.

I remember going through grammar school and men would say things to me that made me sick, but I didn't say a word. I didn't know that I could. I also dealt with the other children being so mean to me; I came from Jamaica to Chicago where I was very different and had a strong accent. America is so different comparison to Jamaica! I would stay during recess to get tutored in English by my peers and every day at recess a bully in the class would undress me by sitting on me and taking off my clothing, giving it back right before the bell would ring for everybody to return from recess. It was so humiliating and traumatic, but once again I felt I had no voice to say no or to tell. A lot of times coming from another country we endure abuse and we stay silent because we don't want to cause any problems, or want to be seen as a problem in this country. I would fight my boy cousins and their friends but, in this instance, wouldn't defend myself. I was so embarrassed as other classmates getting tutored would either join in or watch and do nothing.

From that place, it got harder and harder to stand up for me. Remember until you learn to say no people will continue to play on your frailty. Because predators know who they can prey on and who they cannot. My family would go and visit friends of the family on special occasions and holidays, and I remember this nasty, perverted old man saying things to me that were so inappropriate. At the end of the one of those evenings he would drive me home and I would cringe at the thought because I had to sit there and listen to the perverse things he would say, but because I didn't open my mouth and say something, he took it to another level by choosing to show me porn books and trying to touch me inappropriately. I would make excuses not to be in his presence alone, but one day after going over his house to pick up something for my mom, he decided to drop me home, he proceeded to touch my leg and before he could get to the corner I jumped out of the moving vehicle. I wasn't hurt, I was trying to escape the trap that was set for me, not being able to say no to the open invitation he was giving me.

PART 4

I rest my head on his shoulder today, when he whispered (daughter) softly, I can wipe those tears away; I thank you for the fire that I feel in the depth of my soul, and I know that was truly your goal; so ignite my fire and set me ablaze, that everything that touches me can go up in flames. Fire of Elijah fall on me as I pray and cry for my legacy. the fire of God come to consume our very being, it opens our eyes and causes us to be very keen, the fire of God burns everything in its path, but Jesus you know I don't want to feel God's wrath. I cried loud and he answered and showed me great and mighty things when I decided to bow down/humble myself before the king, I thank you Lord for enduring those lashes, so now I can have beauty for ashes. When the fire come to burn away the things that are blocking its way, cause your people to see and say; Lord, please allow me to see another day; cause tomorrow is not promised and neither is today; so please turn away from those things that easily beset us along the way, many take him for granted and trust only in man, when all he wanted us to say was I CAN; do all things through Christ that strengthen me, and thanks to this fire I now too can see, that my king, my Lord delighteth in me.

Written by Annaliza

The abuse even goes on in our churches now, where pastors and leaders are trusted to watch over our souls but instead, they are using their influence and status to prey on people who are not strong enough to protect themselves.

In business/ministry and in life we are manipulated and raped by leaders who rape us of our time/gifts/talents. They say things that will bring insecurities to you, they do things that bring rejection to you, and the cycle lives on. We must get to a place of being whole. There are leaders who say come preach for me, come sing for me, come dance for me, come prophesy for me, come teach, come help, and it's all to seduce you into doing what they want; then you wonder why you feel so empty and drained.

They just raped you of those gifts, they used you until you were left feeling empty and shameful and used. You didn't see it coming, they use you up and when they are done with you throw you away. Those annihilating spirits are not just sexual, remember I said it could be a word, a touch or penetration. They penetrate your spirit, penetrate your mind, penetrate your soul. Sometimes you need to test the spirit to see if it is of God, everyone is not a part of the kingdom and some people are set on assignment to derail your mandate. They want to suck the anointing from you. Saying, "No" to the invitation, should apply to every area of your life. You can say, "No" to the invitation when people see gift and talents that you possess, and they puff you up and tell you how awesome, gifted and talented you are, so they can manipulate you and steal your voice. When this happens, say, "No!"

It's no different than someone saying oh you're so beautiful, sexy, or commenting on your assets, majority of them want something from you. The Bible says to seek first the kingdom of heaven and all its righteousness and everything else will be added to you. Seek God and follow the unction of the Holy Spirit. Follow the signs and inclination you have in your spirit. When things don't look or feel right, most times they aren't.

All these things happen to destroy your voice, so you won't be the warrior/champion God intended you to be. But the devil is a liar against your destiny. You will be free from every yoke of bondage and everything the enemy meant for bad, God is turning it around for your good right now. Pray, see what God says, and follow that. Remember I spoke about the young prophet that gave that awesome word and the old prophet wanted him to come to his house. He lied to him, deceived him into disobeying God, and he died because of his disobedience.

Disobedience and not being sensitive to the spirit of God can cost you your life, your ministry, your voice, your career, your business, even your marriage. Delayed obedience is disobedience! Everything that looks good isn't always good for you. How many times have you heard stories of a person who obeyed that still small voice and got out the car or plane before an accident? Gods warning always come before destruction. He is faithful to always provide a window of escape.

Often the reason we accept an invitation is the familiar spirit you share. Remember I said if you look back someone may have molested or raped someone in the bloodline. That spirit was never broken and knows who it can prey on or intimidate. We fall prey to people, circumstances, and situations because we draw to the familiar whether good or bad. Kill the cycle now, renounce it if you are the abuser or the victim. Seek help and get to the root of it. This book is not just for the victim but also for the abuser, at some point you were the victim and turned into the abuser. You need to know where the behavior came from, why are you the way that you are, to have a successful future.

Your past is significant, to your healing journey to your freedom. We don't want to deal with our past, but you must in order to be free. Some things we can mask until something triggers the behavior. Stop hiding and be free today.

Before I go any deeper, I want to explain generational curses and the cure to break them. Many people today believe that they are living under spiritual bondage because of the sins of their forefathers.

However,

> *"In those days they shall no longer say:*
> *The fathers have eaten sour grapes, and*
> *the children's teeth are set on edge, but*
> *everyone shall die for his own iniquity."*
>
> *Jeremiah 31: 29- 30, (KJV)*

In other words, once you become a child of God, no longer will you suffer from the sins of your forefathers or parents. Yes, Christ has redeemed us from the curse of the law, being made a curse for us (Galatians 3:13). The legal grounds (generational curse) were certainly paid for on the cross and therefore broken. What believers are likely going through is any bondage or unwanted spirits that were already passed down to them before accepting Jesus Christ. The curse may be canceled, but the demons may remain. There's a profound story in Mark 9:17-27, where Jesus deals with a generational curse (verse 21).

Jesus didn't have the boy to confess the sins or iniquities of his ancestors, He cast out the demons that entered him through the curse. You must cast out those demons that wish to follow you. Therefore, I recommend that you use this strategy to deal with the effects of a generational curse.

Many times, in life we wonder where the behaviors and cycles come from and a lot of it is dated back to when your forefathers and mothers were sold into slavery where they were raped and stripped of their voices. Their blood is crying out, the spirit of murder and rape. The spirit of man was killed which further perpetuated a cycle of death. The blood is crying out, that's why the enemy still has grounds to enter our lives. Have you ever wondered why you have the abused woman syndrome, where you continue to go back to the same system/people that have abused you? In the days of slavery, the slave master could rape you, and when he was finished you still had to go cook his food, take care of his house and family.

The same thing applies here, that spirit is still there it has just taken a different form. You are still broken and stripped, but still feeling that you are indebted, and this is how you must live to survive. This applies to our men as well. Some of them are so nonchalant about things because while their women were being raped, they had to watch and turn their head in fear of losing their lives. They have dealt with words that tell them they are nothing and will never be anything, inviting those things into your ear gates can transform your mindset. Lingering spirit has produced women who are mad at our men for not protecting or providing for us, and men running around having sex with multiple women because of the spirit that stole their manhood. Women we are emotional beings that require emotional stimulation, or we just want to tell you how we feel. It's a cry to be heard! Can you hear our cry? Can you feel our pain?

Once you go to the source of the behavior it's time to kill it at the root. Stop running back to the thing or the person that continues to strip you of your voice, strip you of your freedom! You are no longer enslaved or chained to your pain and suffering. God died so you can be free, you are free, walk in your freedom. He whom the son sets free is free indeed, God became the curse, so you didn't have to. When He died on that cross it was for your victory, it was for your joy, it was for your peace, it was for you to live whole.

Remember,

"Beloved, never avenge yourselves, but leave it to the wrath of God, for it is written, "Vengeance is mine, I will repay, says the Lord."

Romans 12:19 (KJV)

The battle is not yours. Allow God to fight your wars, so you will come out victorious!

I pray that after reading this book, that your eyes would be opened to things that might have been done to you. My desire for you is; that God answer your prayers and bring you to a place called healed. Break every cycle and chain in your life and bring you to a place where you understand you have a right to say yes or no. Most importantly, no one should have the power or the authority over your body or mind to manipulate you into doing something you don't want to do. Also, I pray the Lord will be a hedge of protection over you and your family.

(*Psalms 91*)

"*My voice is gone, and no one can hear me, and now I come to thee, Father set me free from all these things that came to kill me, I am healed and I am free because you came and died for me. I open my mouth and now I can speak to tell of my greatest defeat, but I am stronger and wiser now; when others come to ask me how. Did you stand and conquer this, I did it with fasting and prayer too and come on girl/boy you can do it too!*"

Written by Annaliza

CULMINATION

For those of you reading this, no matter what you have done, God can heal, God can restore, God can set you free!

My desire is for you to be free today. Remember the weapons of our warfare are not carnal but mighty through God to the pulling down of every stronghold. Remember this spirit comes to steal, kill and destroy your life, joy and peace. The enemy uses this thing to bring about fear, low self-esteem/insecurities and cause you to feel worthless; the enemy knows from inception what you are to become and if he can destroy and derail those plans early in life, that's what he will do.

We are overcomers to him that believe. Because no matter what happened to you in your past, God can redeem the time and heal every violated place in your body, in your mind, and in your spirit. He became freedom for me, and you too can be set free from every curse the enemy tries to plague you with. Your liberation and freedom are truly in you making the choice to never be bound again. Take your voice back.

MY PRAYER FOR YOU...

"Father in the name of Jesus, whose name is above every other name, I come today on behalf of everyone reading this book; father I release the angel of the Lord to bring healing and deliverance to those who need it; and father bring awareness to the person who is trying to forget about their past, father for the ones that are going from relationship to relationship, from one bed to the other, struggling with their identity and their sexuality, father deliver them and set them free from every yoke of bondage. Father for the person who blames themselves, God I pray that you would heal their mind; cause them to forgive themselves, even though they were not at fault, teach them how to love again,

teach them how trust again, father set them free from every stronghold, and every trap and snare of the enemy, and every bondage imposed on them by the wrong invitation, father we invite you in to mend all these scars. We say no to every ungodly invitation, and we stand boldly today and say whom the son sets free is free indeed. Let their yes be yes and their no be no. Give them boldness to speak up for themselves. I pray that they will overcome the trauma that they faced by the words that were spoken, the inappropriate touch that they felt, the rape that was forced upon them, as well as overcoming by the blood of the lamb and the words of my testimony. You said you have not given us the spirit of fear but of power love and a sound mind. We give it all to you because God, without you we can do nothing. Give us the strength to deal with the memories of our past and give us the boldness to pursue peace, to fight for freedom and God to live for you. Teach us to forgive not for them but for our sanity. Daddy God, as they have completed reading this book have your way, have your way. I decree and declare that now that they have completed this book, it will cause eyes to be opened, and healing and deliverance will take place and you will fight for victory in your life. I pray that you would be made whole, the trauma will be eradicated from your mind, and now you can live again, love again, sing again, teach again, dance again. Also, I pray that you will: 1. Acknowledge the pain, 2. Deal with the pain and forgive those that have inflicted the pain, 3. Get delivered from the pain. 4. Seek help to deal with the pain, and to be set free to be whole in Jesus Christ of Nazareth's wonderful name. Amen."

Made in the USA
Lexington, KY
14 December 2019

58556471R00061